Star Friends
Dream Shield

To the wonderful team at Tiger Tales who
have helped my books reach US readers – LC
To the Children's Ward at St. Mary's Hospital – KB

LITTLE TIGER
An imprint of Little Tiger Press Limited
1 Coda Studios, 189 Munster Road, London SW6 6AW

Imported into the EEA by Penguin Random House Ireland,
Morrison Chambers, 32 Nassau Street, Dublin D02 YH68

A paperback original
First published in Great Britain in 2024

Text copyright © Linda Chapman, 2024
Illustrations © Kim Barnes, 2024

ISBN: 978-1-78895-627-7

The right of Linda Chapman to be identified as the author and Kim Barnes
as the illustrators of this work respectively has been asserted by them
in accordance with the Copyright, Designs and Patents Act, 1988.

All rights reserved.

This book is sold subject to the condition that it shall not, by
way of trade or otherwise, be lent, resold, hired out, or otherwise
circulated without the publisher's prior consent in any form of
binding or cover other than that in which it is published and
without a similar condition including this condition being
imposed upon the subsequent purchaser.

A CIP catalogue record for this book is available from the British Library.

Printed and bound in the UK.

The Forest Stewardship Council® (FSC®) is a global, not-for-profit organization
dedicated to the promotion of responsible forest management worldwide. FSC
defines standards based on agreed principles for responsible forest stewardship
that are supported by environmental, social, and economic stakeholders.
To learn more, visit www.fsc.org

MIX
Paper | Supporting
responsible forestry
FSC® C171272

2 4 6 8 10 9 7 5 3 1

Star Friends
Dream Shield

Linda Chapman
Illustrated by Kim Barnes

LITTLE TIGER
LONDON

London Borough of Enfield	
91200000804463	
Askews & Holts	10-Jan-2024
JF YGN	
ENSOUT	

In the Star World

Three wise animals – a wolf, a badger and a stag – touched noses as they gathered round a pool in the forest. Their fur glittered with stardust. Around them, silvery trees reached up towards the inky-black sky. Hearing a soft hoot, the animals looked up to see a pale shape gliding towards them. Hunter the owl landed on a tree stump, his indigo eyes anxious.

"Thank you for meeting me here, my friends. There is trouble brewing in Westcombe. Someone close to the village has been using dark magic to influence people for their own gain. This person is dangerous, and I am worried for our friends who live there."

The other animals exchanged uneasy looks.

Every so often, young creatures from the Star World travelled down to the human world to look for a boy or a girl who believed in magic to be their Star Friend. After finding the right person, the animal stayed with them for life, teaching them how to connect to the magic current that linked the two worlds, helping them use it for good. Sometimes that meant assisting people with everyday problems, and at other times it meant stopping those who were using dark magic.

"Do our young friends in Westcombe know about the person who is using dark magic?" asked the badger.

"Not yet," replied Hunter. "So far they have only used small amounts of magic to influence people, but their ambitions are growing. Our Star Friends and their Star Animals must stop them."

He swept a wing over the surface of the forest pool. The pool was a window to the human world and, as the animals watched, the glittering water swirled and an image appeared in it of four eleven-year-old girls and four animals in a clearing in a wood. The animals looked like regular woodland creatures apart from their deep indigo eyes.

"Maia and Bracken," said the wolf, her eyes moving first to a girl with shoulder-length dark blond hair who was tickling the fluffy tummy of a fox lying on his back.

"Sita and Willow," said the stag, his eyes resting on a girl with a thick brown plait and gentle eyes who was stroking a fallow deer. His gaze moved on to a girl with chin-length dark curly hair and hazel eyes who was giggling as a red squirrel jumped from one of her shoulders to the other. "Lottie and Juniper. And Ionie and Sorrel," she finished, looking at the girl with a strawberry-blond ponytail who had a tabby wildcat weaving through her legs.

"They have a lot of power between them," said the badger.

"They will need to use all their powers to stop the person who is using dark magic," said Hunter.

"Will it be dangerous?" asked the wolf anxiously.

Hunter nodded gravely. "I believe this will be the most dangerous challenge our young friends have faced yet."

Chapter One

In a corner of her back garden, Maia stuffed a final handful of straw into her old tiger onesie. "There!" she said happily. She had made a head earlier, and now she fixed it to the top of the broom handle inside the onesie. She pulled up the hood with its tiger ears. "My scarecrow is finally finished!"

"It's really good, Maia," said Bracken.

Maia bent down to ruffle his soft head. Tomorrow there was going to be a scarecrow competition in Westcombe as part of the annual garden walkabout. Her dad had said he would get out a ladder and fix her scarecrow to the creeper outside her bedroom window, to make it seem as if it was climbing down the wall after burgling the house.

"Have you finished?" she asked, looking round at Ionie, who was writing the words *SWAG* in black marker on a sack. Maia was going to fix it on to the cat burglar's back. Ionie had been staying at Maia's while her parents were away on a business trip – they were due back that afternoon.

"I have," said Ionie, frowning at the sack. "But the letters look messy. Maybe I should start again?"

"It looks fine. In fact, it's better than that." Maia grinned. "It's *GRRRRRRRR*eat!"

"It's really not," Ionie said. She always liked everything to be perfect.

"You fuss way too much," said Maia, taking the sack from her and using safety pins to attach it to the scarecrow's back. "There, finished. One *PURRR*fect cat burglar."

Sorrel, Ionie's Star Animal, had been lying on the grass in the sun, but now she sat up. "A *cat* burglar?" she said, sounding extremely unimpressed. "Why is your burglar a cat?" She flicked the end of her tabby tail and fixed Maia with an indignant stare.

"It's what humans sometimes call burglars who climb into houses through windows," Ionie explained. "They're burglars who are especially silent, agile and clever – just like cats."

Sorrel looked at Bracken who was chasing butterflies, leaping up in the air and tumbling over in a heap. "Well, I suppose that does make a degree of sense. Cats are infinitely more clever and agile than other animals." She sniffed. "Particularly foxes."

"Did you see me, Maia? I almost caught it that time!" Bracken jumped into Maia's arms, knocking her backwards. "I really nearly did!" She giggled as he licked her nose.

As far as she was concerned, Bracken was the best Star Animal ever! Since becoming his Star Friend, they'd stopped people causing trouble with plant magic and crystal magic and had fought Shades. Shades were evil spirits who could be conjured from the shadows by dark magic. Once they were trapped in everyday objects, they could be put into people's houses where they caused all sorts of problems. Some made people jealous or competitive or angry; others made wishes come true, but in bad ways. Although trying to fight them and send them back to the shadows was scary, it was also very exciting. Maia simply couldn't imagine a life without magic now, and she certainly couldn't imagine a life without Bracken!

"You're both amazing animals," said Ionie, stroking Sorrel.

"Thanks, Ionie," said Bracken happily.

Sorrel rubbed her head against Ionie's legs. "I am, of course, the most amazing."

"Of course you are," whispered Ionie, scooping her up. Sorrel snuggled into her arms and purred. She could be very sharp-tongued, but she adored Ionie.

"I can't wait to see the other scarecrows," said Maia, starting to clear up. It was always fun to go to all the different gardens and look at the scarecrows. There were usually also craft stalls, mini competitions, a refreshments area and a bouncy castle. In the afternoon, the winning scarecrow would be announced. "I wonder whose scarecrow will win."

"Mike Jefferson's judging, isn't he?" Ionie said.

Maia nodded.

Ionie's green eyes sparkled, and suddenly she transformed into a tall middle-aged man with earnest eyes and a balding head. "Once again, I am delighted to be judging the Westcombe Village Scarecrow Competition," she said, perfectly imitating Mike's deep voice.

Maia giggled. It was as if Mike, the head of the school Parent Teacher Association, was suddenly standing in her garden. Ionie had the ability to use magic to disguise herself as other people – a skill that had been very useful in some of their adventures!

Ionie/Mike held out a hand for Maia to shake. "I am delighted to announce that first prize in the Westcombe Village Scarecrow Competition goes to Maia Greene!" She picked an unripe apple off the ground. "Maia, please accept your prize."

"Thank you, oh, thank you for this awesome apple trophy!" said Maia, playing along and pretending to be overwhelmed. "This is such an honour! I want to thank my mum, my dad, my sister Clio, my brother Alfie, all my friends, my next-door neighbours, John and Barbara Holt…"

She broke off as a voice spoke from the other side of the garden fence. "Maia? Did you just call me?"

Ionie squeaked in alarm and transformed back to her usual self while the Star Animals vanished, leaving just a faint swirl of tiny shimmering stars as a woman with curly brown hair looked over the fence.

"Oh, hi, Barbara!" Maia said, hiding her grin. "Sorry. No, I wasn't calling you. I was just playing a game with Ionie."

"Oooh, I like your scarecrow, dear," said Barbara. "A cat burglar. Very clever. John's just finishing ours off before he displays it round the front of the house. What do you think?" She beckoned them over. They stood on tiptoe and peered over the fence. John, Barbara's husband, was putting the finishing touches to a gardener scarecrow. It was wearing dark trousers stuffed into a pair of green wellies, a checked shirt with a sleeveless green jacket over the top and a hat on its head. It had a plastic flowerpot filled with soil under one arm.

Maia grinned. "It looks just like Mr Stanyard."

Mr Stanyard was a very keen gardener who lived on Clay Street. His garden was always overflowing with flowers. Maia loved walking past it, although she didn't like Mr Stanyard much. He was very grumpy and wasn't keen on children, particularly when they accidentally threw balls into his garden.

Barbara chuckled. "And so it should. The jacket, hat and wellies are his."

"Mr Stanyard lent them to you?" said Ionie.

"He did." Barbara saw their surprise. "Peter Stanyard's not that bad," she said with a smile. "His bark's worse than his bite."

Maia heard her mum calling. "Maia! Ionie! Time to leave!"

"We'd better go," she said. "We're off to the meeting about the houses that Mr Hannigan wants to build."

"John and I will see you there." Barbara shook her head, her lips pursing. "That development simply cannot be allowed to go ahead. Desmond Hannigan thinks he can do whatever he likes, but that clifftop is a real beauty spot. It should be left for everyone to enjoy."

Maia nodded. Desmond Hannigan, a local businessman and property developer, had bought some land on a nearby clifftop and planned to build three huge houses on it. The meeting that afternoon in the village hall was for everyone who objected to the plans to get together to discuss ways of stopping him. Maia and Ionie were meeting Lottie and Sita there. They were worried because if Desmond Hannigan did get permission to build the houses, the diggers and other vehicles would access the clifftop by cutting through the beautiful woods where they went to practise magic.

"Maia! Ionie!" her mum called again.

"Coming!" Maia called back.

They said goodbye to Barbara and hurried up the garden. "After the meeting, we're still going to the clearing, aren't we?" Ionie whispered.

"Yep," said Maia, happiness swirling through her. An afternoon with her friends, practising magic. What could be better than that!

Chapter Two

Maia and Ionie ran through the gate on to the driveway at the front of the house. Maia's mum was locking the front door while Maia's dad was fastening Alfie into his buggy.

"How's the scarecrow coming along?" he asked.

"It's ready to go on the wall," said Maia.

A thick creeper covered the brick wall beneath her bedroom window. Barbara and John's house next door had the same creeper and the same style of windows. The two houses were almost identical; the only difference was the colour of the front door.

"I'll put it up when we get back," her dad promised.

They set off with Alfie pointing out everything he saw to the little blue train in his hand.

"Car … dog … tree … 'nother tree…"

At the end of Clay Street, they reached Mr Stanyard's cottage. A sprinkler was spinning round, watering the emerald-green lawn.
A riot of flowers spilled out of the terracotta pots. An old wheelbarrow had been planted up with pink geraniums, and bushes on either side of the driveway had been clipped into peacock shapes. Mr Stanyard was trimming a final few stray twigs, wearing his usual outfit of wellies and a sleeveless gardening jacket. Outside his house, a woman with frizzy brown hair and a round, friendly face was getting into her car. She was holding a big glass jar, the kind that old-fashioned sweets were sometimes sold in.

"Thanks so much for all your help, Peter!" she called. "The pots you gave us to paint worked really well, and this jar is just what we needed." She spotted Maia's family and waved.

Maia waved back. "Hi, Lizzie!" Lizzie was the leader of the village Brownies group

"Got to dash," Lizzie called. "I'm just off to the meeting in the village hall."

"We'll see you there," Dad said.

Mum smiled at Mr Stanyard. "Your garden's looking as beautiful as ever. It always brightens up my day when I pass it."

Mr Stanyard's lined face softened slightly. "Thank you. I try my best."

"You've certainly got the magic touch," said Maia's dad. "Whoa! No, Alfie!" he said quickly, swerving the buggy to one side as Alfie tried to reach out and grab a flower head. "Sorry about that," he said to Mr Stanyard, who had started to frown at Alfie. "Are you coming to the meeting, Peter?"

"No, I've still got a lot to do before the walkabout tomorrow," said Mr Stanyard gruffly. "I'm running a garden stall selling pots."

"I'll make sure we call by tomorrow then," said Mum. "I need some new pots."

They said goodbye and turned on to Brook Street. Trestle tables had been set out for the garden walkabout stalls and chairs had been unloaded on to a wide drive where refreshments would be served, but people had stopped their preparations and were heading to the meeting.

As they got closer to the village hall, Maia and Ionie spotted Sita and Lottie and ran to catch up with them.

"Hi. Are we still going to the clearing after the meeting to do some –" Lottie glanced round to check no one was close enough to overhear – "*magic*?"

"Definitely," said Maia.

"Will you keep teaching us how to conjure magic shields?" Sita whispered to Maia. "I really want to be able to make one."

Maia nodded. They could all use the magic current to do different things. When Lottie connected to it, she became extremely fast and agile, and she also sometimes had premonitions when danger was coming. Sita could calm, soothe, heal and also command people and spirits to obey her, although she found that power scary and only used it when she really had to. Ionie could disguise herself, travel from place to place in the shadows and was also a Spirit Speaker – someone who could command spirits like Shades to return to their own worlds. Maia's abilities were to do with sight – she could use a shiny surface to see things that were happening elsewhere and get glimpses of the past and future, and she had magic dreams that often showed her things that were useful. However, a few months ago, she had also discovered that she could use the current to create invisible shields. For the past week, she'd been trying to teach the others how to make them, too.

"I think I almost managed to make one last time we were in the clearing," said Lottie.

Ionie shrugged. "I don't see why we need to learn about shields. If we need a barrier, Maia can make one."

"What if Maia's not there?" Sita pointed

out. "Like the time I got kidnapped by Auntie Mabel, and she tried to steal Willow."

They all glanced over to where a sweet old lady with grey curly hair was chatting to Maia's mum and dad. *Auntie Mabel.* Maia felt a shiver run down her spine. Maia had always thought Auntie Mabel was really kind but, not long after she and the others became Star Friends, they'd discovered that she was using dark magic to make people unhappy. She knew about Star Magic and wanted to kidnap their Star Animals. Luckily they'd stopped her, and Sita used her powers to make the old lady forget about magic. It seemed to have worked. Auntie Mabel hadn't caused any more problems since then.

"True, it would be good to be able to protect ourselves," said Lottie in a low voice. "I think we should all keep learning how to make shields."

Ionie pulled a face as if she wasn't convinced. "There are loads of people here for the meeting, aren't there?" she said, looking around. Maia had the feeling that she was trying to change the subject. Ionie hadn't managed to create a shield yet, and Maia knew she didn't like it when she wasn't good at doing something. "Look, there's Brad and Nikhil with their parents," Ionie went on. "And Mary from the Copper Kettle."

"And Mike and Ana-Lucia Jefferson," said Sita, nodding towards a middle-aged couple who were ushering people into the hall.

Maia's eyes fell on a boy who looked about eighteen and was lurking behind some parked cars. He had blond hair with a long fringe that fell over his face. Maia frowned. "Isn't that Desmond Hannigan's son, Sam?"

Her big sister, Clio, was working in Desmond Hannigan's café, The Friendly Fish, at the marina during the summer holiday. When Maia had called in with her dad last week, Clio had introduced them to Sam. He hadn't said much, just mumbled a hello, but from the way Clio kept talking about him, Maia had a feeling she'd like them to be more than just friends.

"Why would Sam Hannigan come to this meeting?" said Lottie, puzzled. "It's for people who are *against* the development."

"Maybe he's spying for his dad," Ionie hissed.

They watched as Sam pulled up the hood of his hoody and sidled into the hall, keeping his head down as if he was hoping he wouldn't be recognized.

Suspicious, thought Maia, *definitely suspicious.*

Through the open doors, they heard someone banging a table to get people's attention. "Come on, we'd better go in," she said.

The meeting went on for over an hour. The adults were keen to try to stop the development, and plans were drawn up as to how everyone could protest. They discussed the petitions they were going to sign, the letters they were going to write and the wildlife surveys they were going to organize in the hope of finding an endangered species living on the site that might stop the houses from being built.

Maia sat at the back with Lottie, Sita and Ionie. She understood the meeting was important but she couldn't wait to go to the clearing and was glad when it ended.

Sam Hannigan was the first to slip out of the hall and by the time Maia and the others came out, he had gone. Maia had already told her mum that she and Ionie were going to meet up with the others after the meeting, so they left the chattering crowd and headed down Church Lane towards the main road. They passed a house with a fairy scarecrow outside holding a wand, another with a scarecrow dressed as a pop singer with a blow-up guitar, and outside Lizzie the Brownie leader's house there were three small scarecrows all dressed in Brownie uniforms.

"Have you finished your scarecrows yet?" Maia asked Lottie and Sita.

They both nodded. "Mine's a doctor." Lottie took out her phone and showed Maia a photo of a scarecrow dressed in a white coat with a stethoscope around its neck.

"And mine's a Bollywood dancer," said Sita, producing a photo of a scarecrow wearing a wig and one of her gran's bright saris.

"They're great," said Maia, smiling. "I'll send you a picture of mine later."

"I hope one of you wins the competition," said Ionie.

"I don't really care if I win or not," said Sita, pushing her plait over her shoulder. "It's making them that's the fun thing, isn't it?"

Maia nodded in agreement.

"Winning's even more fun." Lottie pointed to the end of the street where the main road was. "Race you to the street sign? On your marks, get set … GO!"

Maia dashed after her with Sita, though they knew neither of them stood a chance of catching up. Even without using magic, Lottie was the fastest out of all of them. She was just about to touch the street sign when Ionie suddenly appeared in the shadow of the wall beside it and hit it with her hand.

"Beat you!" she said.

"That's not fair!" cried Lottie indignantly.

"Why not? You didn't say we couldn't use magic," said Ionie.

Lottie crossed her arms. "If I'd used magic, I could have beaten you!"

"I don't think—"

"Don't start arguing, you two," Maia said quickly, knowing that if Ionie and Lottie began to quarrel it could go on for ages. She checked the main road. It was clear of traffic. "Come on," she said, starting to cross it with Sita. "You want to do magic, don't you?"

Lottie and Ionie forgot their argument. "Yes!" they exclaimed, running after them.

Chapter Three

The four girls burst into the clearing, calling their animals, who appeared in a shimmer of tiny silver stars. Trees were clustered round a circle of lush grass, which was dotted with wildflowers. At the edges of the clearing, swathes of tall cow parsley stood, their large creamy-white flower heads as wide as saucers. Bees buzzed from flower to flower, and yellow butterflies danced through the air. In the centre of the clearing, there was a small waterfall, the water tumbling down over rocks and flowing away in a sparkling stream towards the sea.

Maia's heart sang. She loved the beautiful clearing. *We absolutely can't let Desmond Hannigan bring diggers through here*, she thought.

"Let's do magic!" said Bracken, bounding round her.

"Hey, everyone!" Maia called. "Do you want to have a go at making magical shields again?"

Sita and Lottie grinned and hurried over with Juniper and Willow. Ionie joined them more reluctantly.

"Remember what I told you last time," said Maia. "Connect with the current just like you usually do and then imagine pulling an invisible sheet from the ground. Pull it up until it's covering you. That's it!"

"If you stroke your animals, that might help," added Bracken. Connecting to the magic current was always easier when the girls were touching their Star Animals.

Maia watched her friends as they settled

down, their foreheads creased in concentration.

"I think I'm doing it," breathed Lottie suddenly.

"Ooh, me too!" said Sita.

Maia could see a faint glimmer forming round them both, almost like they had giant translucent bubbles covering them. Other people couldn't see the bubbles but Maia's magic abilities allowed her to see things they couldn't.

She picked up a small stick and tossed it towards Lottie. The stick hit the magic shield and bounced back. "Yay! You've got it!" She threw a pine cone at Sita. It also pinged away. "You too, Sita."

"How about Ionie?" Bracken said eagerly.

Maia turned to where Ionie, with Sorrel on her lap, was frowning deeply. "I can do this! I can!" she was muttering.

"Ionie, I think you're maybe trying too hard," suggested Maia. "If you relax and—"

Ionie threw up her hands. "Maia, I can't concentrate with you talking all the time!"

"I was only trying to help," Maia protested.

"Well, you ruined it," said Ionie crossly. "I'd have been able to do it if you hadn't started talking." She jumped to her feet. "I'm going to use my magic for something else." Suddenly she transformed into grumpy gardener, Mr Stanyard, complete with hat and wellies. "What are you children doing here? Standing on the grass, bending the stalks. You'll be touching a flower next, if I know you!"

Maia grinned as Ionie stomped around, perfectly imitating Mr Stanyard. "Children! Pah! They cycle on my grass verge and throw balls that hit my flowers. They should be in school twenty-four hours a day, all year round!" She shook her fist at them. "Go on! Clear off!"

Sita and Lottie giggled, letting their magic shields fade. "You're brilliant at glamours, Ionie," said Sita.

"Ionie? Who's Ionie?" said Ionie, and she transformed again, this time becoming Auntie Mabel. She tottered towards them, rubbing her hands. "Now, girls, you really have been very mean not letting me use crystal magic to cause trouble. I do think you should give me one of those Star Animals of yours." Her voice changed to a sinister hiss. "*Give them to me or I'll use my crystals to conjure SHADES!*"

At that, she transformed into a Shade, her body becoming tall and thin, her hands and fingers elongating, her nails turning to claws and her eyes becoming red slits. The others shrieked and scattered. Even though they knew it was Ionie, she looked so like a Shade, it was hard not to feel scared.

Ionie burst out laughing and changed back into herself. "Your faces! You looked terrified."

"You're too good at transforming yourself," said Maia, her heart rate gradually slowing down.

"Really, really good," Lottie said.

Ionie looked smug.

"Exceptional," purred Sorrel, weaving round her legs. "You are incredibly talented at doing magic, Ionie."

Apart from conjuring magic shields, Maia thought, wondering if Ionie had used glamours to hide the fact she couldn't make a shield like they all could.

"Someone's coming!" Willow said suddenly, her ears flicking.

The animals vanished as the cow parsley at the end of the overgrown footpath that led into the clearing was pushed aside and a young woman stepped through it. Her braided black hair was tied back in a thick ponytail. Her brown eyes lit up when she saw the girls, and she waved.

"Hi, Miss Amadi," they chorused, relaxing and calling their animals back.

Miss Amadi was a Star Friend with a Star Otter called Fen. She had been Maia and Ionie's teacher for their last term at primary school. Although they were starting secondary school in September, they all agreed that calling her by her first name – Ginni – would be too weird.

"Hi, girls. I was hoping I might find you here," she said. "I'd love some more help trying to use my healing magic."

When Miss Amadi had revealed to the girls

that she was a Star Friend, she had told them she didn't know much about Star Magic. She and Fen hadn't had a group of friends to learn with when they were younger. The girls and their animals had been helping them ever since.

"Of course," said Sita. Miss Amadi had soothing and healing magic like her, although she didn't have Sita's power to command people and spirits.

Miss Amadi whistled and Fen appeared. She had sparkling indigo eyes and long whiskers. Miss Amadi crouched down, and Fen gave her a whiskery kiss on the nose.

"I've been practising my magic every day," Miss Amadi said. "I can make wilted and damaged plants healthy again but I haven't managed to heal many humans yet." A smile tugged at the corners of her lips. "It's not that easy to find people to practise on."

"I've got a scratch," said Lottie, holding out her arm. "You could practise on me."

"That would be great!" said Miss Amadi enthusiastically. "Sita, maybe you can give me some tips on controlling my healing magic? I find that sometimes it works and sometimes it doesn't."

Lottie, Sita and Miss Amadi sat down on the grass together.

Ionie began amusing herself by shadow-travelling between the trees. She stepped into one patch of shadows and appeared in another on the opposite side of the clearing.

Maia also decided to do some magic. She took out the pocket mirror she always carried with her and sat down with it cradled in her hands. Bracken rested his chin on her leg, and Maia connected to the current. It was as easy for her now as turning on a light switch. "Show me what's happening in Westcombe," she whispered.

The surface of the mirror swirled, and a series of images appeared: Maia's house with her dad fixing the cat burglar to the creeper under her bedroom window; Brook Street where the final few stalls were being set up; the village hall where Mike Jefferson and some other villagers were putting up bunting; and the Hall Farm field where people were unloading a bouncy castle out of a van.

"Everything seems completely normal," she told Bracken.

"Try looking into the future," he suggested.

"OK." She shut her eyes and focused her mind. "Show me something that's *going to happen in Westcombe*."

Opening her eyes, she saw a picture of the whole village with black clouds covering it.

"Whoa!" she said and quickly told Bracken. "Do you think it means there's going to be a storm?"

"Maybe." Bracken looked troubled. "Or maybe the cloud is dark magic."

Maia felt her stomach flip.

There was a burst of clapping from the other side of the clearing.

"Maia! Ionie! Miss Amadi just healed Lottie's scratch!" Sita called. She frowned, seeing the expression on Maia's face. "Maia? Are you OK?"

"I've seen something with my magic," Maia said, going over. "And I don't think it's good." She told the others what she'd seen.

"So you think it means bad magic is coming to Westcombe," said Sita, her eyes wide.

"What kind?" said Lottie.

"I don't know," Maia said.

Ionie's eyes flashed with determination. "We've dealt with plant magic, crystal magic, Shades, charms and potions. Whatever it is, we'll find a way of handling it."

Sorrel purred approvingly.

"Fen and I can help, too," said Miss Amadi eagerly.

"From now on let's keep our eyes and ears open. If anyone sees anything suspicious or odd, tell the rest of us because it could be the dark magic starting," Maia said. Her friends and their animals nodded. Maia put her hands on her hips and lifted her chin. "Whoever's thinking of doing something bad in Westcombe had better watch out!"

Chapter Four

When Maia woke up the next morning, Bracken was lying beside her on his back, his legs in the air. She'd forgotten to close her window or shut the curtains and sunlight was streaming in. *It's the garden walkabout today*, she realized, her heart turning a happy somersault as she sat up. Bracken raised his head, his pointed ears pricking.

"Is it time to get up?"

"Yes." Maia glanced at her bedside clock. "I'm meeting the others after breakfast, then we're going to walk round the gardens together and look at the scarecrows. While we're out, we'll keep our eyes peeled for anything unusual."

Shades made people behave oddly or caused strange things to happen. In the past, they had dealt with a Mirror Shade who had made Clio become very jealous of her best friend; Fear Shades who had been hidden in toys and made people think that their worst fears were coming true; Night Shades in dreamcatchers who had made the adults so competitive they'd started hurting each other; and a Wish Shade and Heart's Desire Shades who had made people's wishes come true in horrible ways. They'd also dealt with a magic charm that made people want to eat cake all the time as well as a perfume potion that had made Maddie, one of their classmates, so popular everyone had started fighting to be her friend.

Whatever kind of magic it was, it had to be stopped.

Maia got dressed and tugged a brush through her hair. "I probably won't be able to see you again until this evening, but I'll tell you everything then," she said to Bracken.

He snuffled at her cheek. "Have fun!"

Maia gave him a hug and, feeling light and happy at the thought of the day ahead, she ran downstairs.

"There are loads of people here," said Maia as she and the others walked down Clay Street with their garden walkabout passes. Yellow bunting was fluttering between the lamp posts, and most of the houses they passed had scarecrows next to their gates or in their front gardens. They saw a cricketer scarecrow with a foam bat, a road-maintenance scarecrow with a traffic cone and a conductor with a baton.

People thronged the streets, older village residents strolling in twos and threes, parents pushing buggies and holding on to the hands of skipping toddlers as well as lots of children who

Maia knew from school. The gardens that were open had yellow balloons tied to their gateposts, and there was a map to show which houses had scarecrows to look at.

The girls came to Mr Stanyard's house. Although he hadn't made a scarecrow, there were lots of people in his garden admiring the flowers and queueing up to buy garden pots.

At the stall being run by the Brownies and Guides, they spent some of their money entering a competition to guess how many sweets there were in a big glass jar.

"Help yourselves to a plant, girls," Lizzie, the Brownie leader, said, waving at the tabletop covered with small painted flowerpots filled with soil, tiny plants and a flag with a message on. "Mr Stanyard gave us the pots, and the Brownies painted them and planted the seedlings. We're giving them out for free."

Maia read aloud the message on one of the flags:

Water me and in a while I will bloom and make you smile!

She grinned. "That's nice! We'd better not take them now though; they might get broken as we walk around."

"No problem but do come back later," Lizzie said. "I'm sure there'll be some left."

They said goodbye and went on to the next stall where Auntie Mabel and a couple of ladies from church were selling little animals made out of pine cones. Miss Amadi was there, buying a hedgehog.

"Hi, girls," she said. "I wish I'd known this walkabout was such a big thing – I'd have made a scarecrow and joined in. Are you going to buy an animal? They're really cute."

"And all the proceeds go to village funds," said Auntie Mabel, beaming at them with her twinkly blue eyes.

The girls fished out their purses and bought one each. Maia had just put hers in her bag when she heard their names being called. She saw Maddie Taylor waving at them from a table by the refreshments stall where she was sitting with her mum. "It's Maddie," she said. "Let's go and say hi."

Maddie and her mum had only moved to Westcombe a few months ago. Maddie had found it hard to make friends at first, but now she was settling in. Maia really liked her and secretly hoped that one day another Star Animal might come along so Maddie could practise magic with them.

"We've seen your scarecrows. They're all really good," Maddie said as Maia and the others stopped by her table.

"Did you make one, Maddie?" Sita asked.

"No, we only just got back from holiday. I didn't have time."

"We were hoping we'd see you, girls," said Mrs Taylor. "The weather's so hot, I'm going to take Maddie to the water park tomorrow. Do you want to come along? If you do, I can have a word with your parents."

"That would be great," said Maia, looking round at the others who nodded.

"We'd love to go," said Lottie.

"Wonderful! I'll speak to your parents and pick you up in the morning," said Mrs Taylor. She got to her feet, picking up a couple of plant pots from beside her chair. "Come on, Mads, we'd better not hog this table. There are people waiting to sit down. Let's drop these pots at home and go and look round some more."

Maddie beamed. "I'll see you all tomorrow!"

"The water park – yay!" said Lottie as Maddie and her mum left. The inflatable obstacle course was brilliant fun, and they hadn't been there yet this summer.

"I love going on the slides," said Maia happily.

They headed for the cake stall. Mary from the Copper Kettle had donated the cakes, and Maia's mum was serving, along with Sita's gran. The girls chose a cupcake each and ate them as they walked round the village, looking at the scarecrows.

They had a great time. After they'd visited all the gardens, they played on the bouncy castle in the field. For lunch they had hot dogs, then they got ice creams from the ice-cream van and sat under a weeping willow tree by the brook while the raffle was drawn and Mike Jefferson announced the winning scarecrow.

Lizzie won it with her three Brownie scarecrows. Lottie and Ionie were a bit disappointed but Maia and Sita didn't care.

"Lizzie's scarecrows were really good," said Maia. "And she did have three of them."

"Look!" said Ionie, nodding to where a smartly dressed man with slicked-back greying hair, sharp eyes and shiny shoes was coming from the direction of the car park. A blond woman wearing a smart dress was holding on to his arm. "It's Desmond Hannigan, the one who wants to build those houses."

"That must be his wife," said Lottie, looking at the woman. Maia spotted Sam Hannigan, Desmond's son, walking a little way behind them. His hands were buried in his pockets, his shoulders slumped and his eyes staring at the ground. He looked like he didn't want to be there.

Other people had noticed the Hannigans, too, and were whispering and nudging each other, sending Desmond Hannigan annoyed looks. His plans to build houses on the clifftop definitely didn't make him a popular person in Westcombe at the moment.

"Mr Hannigan!" Maia saw Mike Jefferson step down from the platform where he'd just announced the scarecrow winner. "Hello."

"It was such a nice day we thought we'd stop by and have a stroll around," said Mr Hannigan.

"Dezzie, you didn't tell me there'd be walking," his wife complained.

Desmond patted his wife's hand. "Mike, this is my wife, Tanya. Tanya, this is Mike Jefferson, chair of Westcombe school's Parent Teacher Association."

Tanya Hannigan haughtily extended her

hand almost as if she expected Mike to kiss it.

Maia saw Mike's surprised look. Raising his eyebrows slightly, he shook it instead and then turned back to Desmond. "I'm glad we've bumped into each other, Desmond. There was a meeting in the village hall yesterday, and there's a lot of unhappiness about your proposed development. People in Westcombe really don't want houses built on the clifftop. It's an area of great beauty. Won't you reconsider?"

"Reconsider? Absolutely not!" said Mr Hannigan with a snort. "And I've already heard about that meeting." He glanced at his son who quickly looked away.

"I told you Sam was spying," Ionie hissed to the others.

"I'm going ahead with the development whether the people here like it or not," Mr Hannigan snapped.

Mike frowned. "I warn you, the village is not going to give up without a fight."

Mr Hannigan poked him in the chest with a long finger. "And I warn you that those houses are going to be built. The council's meeting next week, and I can tell you right now that the plans will be approved. Come on, Tanya," he said, turning round. "I've changed my mind about that stroll."

He marched away with Tanya beside him. Maia saw Sam roll his eyes and head after them.

"He's such a horrible man!" Sita burst out. "He doesn't care at all about the wildlife whose homes he'll be ripping up or the trees and plants he'll be destroying."

Maia squeezed her arm. It was very unusual for Sita to get angry about anything. "I know. I hope the adults manage to stop him."

"I wish we could do something with magic," said Ionie.

Maia wished that, too, but it would be wrong to use magic against Mr Hannigan. Things would be different if he was using dark magic himself but he was just a businessman, wanting to make money. "We can't."

"Why not? Sita could use her magic to command him not to build them," Ionie said.

"No!" Lottie, Maia and Sita said at the same time.

"Ionie! That would be really wrong!" said Lottie, shocked.

"I do want to save the clifftop but not by using my magic like that," said Sita.

Ionie huffed. "OK, it was only an idea."

Maia jumped to her feet, keen to stop a row. "I'm thirsty – let's get a drink."

They bought glasses of squash and sat at a table to drink them. Sita got out her pine-cone mouse with its shining eyes and long tail. "This is so cute!"

Maia and Lottie pulled out their animals, too –

Maia had bought a
hedgehog and Lottie
a squirrel. Ionie's face
fell as she checked her
pockets. "Oh no, I think
I've dropped mine somewhere."

"Should we go and see if there are any left?" said Maia.

Ionie nodded but when they got to the stall they found that all the animals had been sold, and Auntie Mabel was clearing away. "I haven't got any more but don't be upset, dear," she said to Ionie when she heard Ionie had lost hers. "I'll make you another once I've collected some more pine cones, and I'll drop it off at your house. What would you like? A mouse, a hedgehog or a squirrel?"

"A mouse, please," said Ionie, looking much happier. "Thank you!"

"Auntie Mabel's a lot nicer now she's not doing magic any more, isn't she?" Sita whispered as they left the stall. They all grinned.

"Maia! Can you give me a hand taking this stuff home?" Maia's mum was carrying two big bags and a couple of plant pots she'd bought at Mr Stanyard's.

"Sure!" Maia said goodbye to the others and hurried to help her mum. She took one of the bags from her.

Lizzie the Brownie leader was packing up her stall nearby. "Do you want one of the Brownies' plant pots? There are a couple left," she called.

"Thanks, Lizzie," said Maia's mum, taking one of the decorated pots Lizzie was offering. She smiled at Maia. "Now home time. I'm exhausted. I'm thinking takeaway pizza for dinner tonight!"

Maia hooked her hand through her mum's arm. "Sounds good to me!"

Chapter Five

After supper, Maia told Bracken all about her day. He lay beside her, his chin resting on her shoulder and his whiskers tickling her ear.

"Did you see anything strange or anyone behaving oddly?" he asked.

"No, nothing," said Maia.

"Perhaps your dreams will tell you something more," said Bracken. Maia often had magic dreams when dark magic was being used.

Maia yawned. "I don't think I'm going

to dream of anything tonight. I'm way too tired." She kissed him and turned out her light. "Night, Bracken. Remember to disappear if Mum or Dad looks in."

"I always do," he said, giving her nose a quick lick before moving to the end of the bed where he curled up at Maia's feet.

She wriggled her toes, smiling as she felt his warm, comforting weight and, seconds later, she was asleep.

Maia looked round. She was in Westcombe at night, not far from her home. The streets were empty, curtains drawn in houses, and the only light came from the orange glow of the lamp posts. There was a dark figure a little further down the street wearing a long coat with a hood. As Maia watched, they paused briefly in a driveway and then hurried on a few houses and stopped again.

What's that person doing? Maia thought as the night breeze whispered across the bare skin of her arms. A feeling of foreboding prickled down her spine. She approached the person but, no matter how quickly she went, she couldn't catch up with them. Turning a corner, she found herself in her own street.

The dark figure stopped by John and Barbara's house and then looked up at Maia's window. Maia edged closer. What were they up to? Why were they here? Suddenly she heard a heavy footstep behind her. She swung round and cried out in surprise as she saw a plant pot swinging towards her head.

"They must be stopped!" a dry, scratchy voice hissed. And then the world went black.

Maia woke up with a start. Bracken was licking her cheek. "Maia, are you OK? You were calling out."

Maia's heart was beating fast. "I was having a dream. A magic dream, I'm sure of it." She told him what she'd seen.

Bracken looked worried. "I wonder what it meant. Who must be stopped?"

Maia stroked him. "I'll tell the others about it in the morning. Maybe it means that the dark magic *has* come to Westcombe." She shivered. "I'm not sure I want to go back to sleep again."

"Don't worry, I'm here," said Bracken, cuddling up to her. "I'll wake you if it looks like you're having another bad dream."

Maia lay down again, hugging him, and after a while her breathing slowed and her eyes closed. This time her dreams were far more relaxing. She dreamed she was floating in a turquoise blue swimming pool, and then she was swinging in a hammock under an oak tree before lying in long, soft grass in a flower-filled meadow...

She was woken up by her phone alarm going off. She groaned and reached to switch it off. "I don't want to wake up – my dreams are too nice."

Bracken had moved to the end of the bed. He looked up, his face relieved. "No more bad dreams then?"

"None," said Maia. She flopped back against her pillows. *I could sleep a little bit longer*, she thought. She felt very tempted – her bed was so comfy.

"Aren't you getting up?" Bracken said in surprise.

"Not yet," said Maia, closing her eyes.

"But don't you have to get ready to go swimming with Maddie this morning?" Bracken said.

Maia realized he was right. Maddie's mum had arranged to collect them at 9.30 a.m. – in half an hour. She needed to have breakfast and get her swim things ready.

With a sigh, she flung back the duvet and got up. She'd left her window open, and a couple of leaves from the creeper had blown in. She threw them back out of the window and pulled on her clothes.

"Make sure you tell the others about your magic dream," said Bracken.

"I will," promised Maia.

When she went downstairs, she was surprised to find the kitchen deserted and the rest of her family still asleep. It wasn't unusual for Clio to still be in bed at 9 a.m. but Maia couldn't remember the last time her mum and dad had had a lie-in. Alfie was usually up by six o'clock!

She went back upstairs to wake her mum up. "Goodness, is that the time?" her mum said sleepily as she checked her phone. "Yesterday must have completely tired me out. David, time to get up," she said, gently shaking Maia's dad's shoulder. "You've got that meeting about the new houses in an hour."

Maia's dad buried his face further in the pillow.

"I'll get him some coffee," Maia's mum said.

She got out of bed, fetched a sleepy Alfie from his room and then knocked on Clio's door. "Clio, time to get up or you'll be late for work."

Maia waited for her sister's shriek as she realized she'd overslept and didn't have time to spend an hour doing her make-up and hair, but instead she just heard her groan. "I'm too tired to work today, Mum. I'm going to phone in sick."

"Oh no, you're not," said Mum, handing Alfie to Maia. He rested his sleepy head against her shoulder as her mum went into Clio's room, opened the curtains and tweaked back the duvet. "Up you get."

Complaining bitterly, Clio dragged herself out of bed.

Maia went downstairs with them and got herself a bowl of cereal, but despite her long sleep she still felt so tired she could barely be bothered to eat it. Her mum and Alfie seemed to feel the same.

Alfie threw his toast soldiers on the floor. "My don't want!" he whined. "My want to sleep."

"I feel the same." Maia's mum felt his forehead. "I wonder if we're coming down with a bug," she said. "Come on, sweetie." She lifted him out of his highchair. "Let's go and watch some cartoons together."

Maia packed a towel and a swimsuit and sat outside on the doorstep, waiting for Maddie's mum. The cat burglar had slipped down the creeper, and there were some leaves scattered on the driveway beneath it.

I should probably pick those up, Maia thought. But she couldn't be bothered.

She looked over at John and Barbara's house. The rake beside their scarecrow had fallen over.

A large blue car drew up. "Maia! Hi!" called Maddie, putting down the window.

Ionie waved from the seat behind her and opened the door. Lottie and Sita were sitting in a third row of seats at the very back.

"Hi, Maia," said Mrs Taylor brightly. "How are you this morning?"

"OK, just a bit tired," said Maia, shutting the door and sinking gratefully into her seat.

Ionie rolled her eyes. "Not you as well. Sita and Lottie have been half asleep since we picked them up."

"Sorry," said Sita, trying to smile.

Lottie yawned. "I don't know why I feel so exhausted."

Mrs Taylor chuckled. "Hopefully the water park will soon wake you all up!"

Chapter Six

Maia usually loved playing on the giant inflatable obstacle course with slides and giant floating pillows but that day she didn't seem to have a scrap of energy.

Sita and Lottie joined her. "I just can't swim any more," said Lottie as Maddie, her mum and Ionie flew down the biggest slide, shrieking with laughter. "I don't know what's up with me."

"We must have the same bug," said Maia. "I bet we caught it at the walkabout."

"How come Ionie didn't get it, too?" said Lottie.

Maia shrugged.

"I feel really bad we're not out there with Maddie," said Sita. "It was really nice of her mum to bring us here."

They nodded in agreement but none of them moved.

Luckily Mrs Taylor was very understanding when she, Ionie and Maddie got out. "You poor things," she said. "Let's get some lunch and see if that helps."

But nothing shifted the tiredness Maia was feeling — not lunch nor ice-cream sodas at the café — and she felt very relieved when they finally set off for home.

"It's quiet in the village today, isn't it?" Ionie said when they got back to Westcombe.

In the summer holidays, there would usually be people walking dogs, children out on bikes, toddlers feeding the ducks and residents sitting on the village benches, but today there were only a few people to be seen. Mr Stanyard was sweeping his drive and Miss Amadi was cleaning her windows.

"I guess everyone's recovering after yesterday," said Mrs Taylor.

"I'm really sorry we've been a bit out of it today," Maia said when they stopped at her house. "When we're feeling better, Maddie, do you want to come round to mine for a sleepover?"

Maddie's face lit up. "That would be brilliant. Yes, please!"

"I hope you get well soon, Maia," said Mrs Taylor as Maia got out.

"Thanks." She waved them off and headed thankfully back into the house. All she wanted to do was collapse in bed.

Her dad was sitting in the kitchen, half-heartedly reading a book while Alfie played listlessly with some trains on the floor.

"Where's Mum?" asked Maia.

"In the study, trying to do some work," said Dad. "We're all feeling a bit rotten. I had to miss the meeting about the new houses this morning. How are you feeling?"

"Not great," Maia admitted. "I'm going upstairs to have a rest."

As soon as she was in her bedroom, she called Bracken.

"Hi! How was today?" he said, bouncing round her.

"Not great. I feel so tired." Closing her eyes, she flopped back on the duvet.

"Tired?" Bracken echoed in surprise. "But you had loads of sleep last night." He jumped up beside her and lay on her tummy, his paws and nose by her face. "You're not tired really, Maia. You're not! Let's do some magic!"

"I can't," Maia groaned.

"Please. *Pleeeeease!*"

Maia stroked his soft fur and after a few minutes she began to feel a bit more awake. "I am actually starting to feel a bit better," she said, sitting up.

"What did the others think when you told them about your dream?" said Bracken.

Maia's hand flew to her mouth. "I didn't tell them!"

"You forgot?" Bracken said in astonishment.

"I was just feeling so sleepy." She took her phone out. "I'll text them now." She sent a message:

> Need to talk to u all.
> I had a dream last night.
> Can we have a call? Mx

She ended with a star, praying hands and a hopeful face emoji, hoping the others would realize she meant a magic dream. They never put too much in texts about magic in case one of their parents read their messages.

The replies pinged back.

> Sure. When? Ix

> There's something I need to tell you, too. Sxxx

> I'm free now 👍 Lxx

Maia shifted position so she was sitting cross-legged with Bracken on her lap and called her friends.

One by one, they answered until the four of them were all on the screen together. Maia could see their animals, too — Sita was sitting on the floor with Willow curled up beside her, Juniper was on Lottie's shoulder, playing with her hair, and Sorrel was perched next to Ionie on her bed.

"How are you all feeling?" Ionie asked.

"A bit better now," said Maia. Lottie and Sita nodded as well.

"So what was your dream about, Maia?" asked Lottie.

Maia explained.

"Was the person you followed a man or a woman?" Ionie asked.

"I don't know. I just saw them from behind."

"I can't believe you didn't tell us about this sooner," Ionie said.

"I'm sorry. I was feeling so tired, I forgot," said Maia.

"Actually, I should also have told you I had one of my weird feelings this morning," Lottie admitted. "The kind of feeling I get when something bad is about to happen."

Willow nudged Sita. "There's something I should have told you all, too," Sita said. "Willow thought she smelled a Shade this morning when I got up." Willow and Sorrel could both smell when Shades had been close by.

"Seriously?" Ionie exclaimed. "Lottie had one of her weird feelings, Willow thought she smelled a Shade, Maia had a magic dream and not one of you thought to mention any of these things?"

Maia blushed and noticed Lottie and Sita looking shame-faced, too. "It's this bug. It's making my mind really foggy. You're lucky you haven't got it."

"Maia, why don't you ask your magic to show you the Shade?" suggested Bracken.

Maia took out her mirror. Letting herself connect to the magic current, she said, "Show me the Shade Willow smelled this morning."

The surface became a swirling black cloud. Maia blinked. "I can't see anything, just a black cloud. It's like when someone uses magic to block me from seeing them. Wait, the cloud's getting darker."

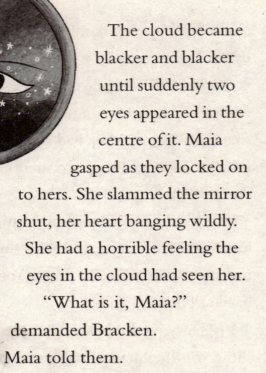

The cloud became blacker and blacker until suddenly two eyes appeared in the centre of it. Maia gasped as they locked on to hers. She slammed the mirror shut, her heart banging wildly. She had a horrible feeling the eyes in the cloud had seen her.

"What is it, Maia?" demanded Bracken.

Maia told them.

Her friends' expressions turned to alarm. "Have you ever seen eyes like that before when you've been using your magic?" asked Lottie.

"No," said Maia.

Ionie took a breath. "Something strange is definitely going on."

"Your dreams may show you more tonight," said Bracken.

"I promise I'll tell you all if they do," said Maia.

They agreed to meet the next day and ended the call. Maia sat for a moment on her bed, stroking Bracken. "I don't think I want to go to sleep tonight."

His gaze met hers. "I'll be here. I'll wake you if I think you're having a bad dream, and you may find out something useful."

Maia felt a bit better. "I guess so. Promise you won't leave me?"

Bracken cuddled down beside her. "Only if your parents look in, and I'll come right back!"

Maia fell asleep quickly that night. She found herself in a garden in the dark, standing beside a fence. She stiffened. It was her back garden, and a man was leaning inside one of the open downstairs windows. He was wearing wellies and a hat. What was he doing? Maia started to edge along the fence to her left, wanting to get closer. She thought he looked familiar.

Before she could work out who the man was, she heard a rustle on the other side of the fence. She froze. It sounded like an animal – a big one – was creeping up on her. Her scalp prickled. *Get inside!* she thought. She started to run but suddenly she wasn't heading towards her house, she was charging down a street. There were feet pounding behind her. Glancing over her shoulder, she saw a shadowy mob of people chasing her with weapons in their hands. A large animal was bounding beside them. Maia skidded round a corner and found another mob coming in the other direction. They lumbered towards her, yelling and waving objects. There was something very strange about the way they were moving and the weapons they were holding, but she didn't have time to think about it. A plant pot whizzed through the air, just missing her head. She cried out in alarm as it hit the ground and the people thundered closer…

⭐⭐⭐

Maia woke up, sitting bolt upright, her hair sticking to her face. Bracken was beside her, pawing at her arm. "Are you OK, Maia? Were you having a magic dream?"

She pushed her hair back. Her heart was pounding. "Yes." She took a trembling breath, starting to calm down as she cuddled Bracken.

"It was really scary." She told him about it.

"Something's definitely going on," he said anxiously. "It sounds like you saw people in Westcombe being affected by some kind of dark magic."

"But what kind?" Maia said.

"I don't know. Let's find out more when we meet the others tomorrow." He looked at the moon shining outside the half-open window. "It's still night-time now. Try to get some sleep."

"I don't think I'll be able to," said Maia, but even as she spoke she yawned and a wave of tiredness washed over her. "Maybe I'll just shut my eyes for a while."

A few moments later, she had fallen asleep.

Maia was woken from a dream of snoozing in a sunny meadow by Bracken snuffling her face with his cold, damp nose. "Bracken!

Get off!" she groaned, opening her eyes and then shutting them again. "It's too early."

"It's not. It's past nine o'clock. I've been waiting for you to wake up for ages, and your phone's been buzzing."

Maia reached for her phone and squinted at it. "It's just Ionie." There were three messages.

> Hi. How r u? Any better? Did u dream again? Ix

> Maia? Are u there? Ix

> Maia, why aren't u answering me?

Maia put her phone down. She'd answer later. Now she just wanted to sleep. She turned over in bed, pulling the duvet round her.

"Maia, what are you doing?" said Bracken, licking her hand. "Don't go to sleep again!"

"I'm too tired to get up." Her phone buzzed and she groaned. "What now?"

Bracken picked it up and dropped it on her hand. "Read it. It could be important."

Maia opened one eye and saw another message from Ionie:

> MAIA! STOP IGNORING ME!!!!!!!!

She pushed the phone away. "It's really not."

Pulling her pillow over her head, she fell back to sleep.

She was dreaming of lying on a sandy beach when she heard a crash. She woke up and sat bolt upright as Ionie stumbled out of the shadows beside her wardrobe, nearly tripping over Maia's tennis racquet and new hockey stick. Sorrel leaped over them lightly.

Ionie had her phone in her hand. "What are you still doing in bed, Maia? Why aren't you answering my texts?"

"It's first thing in the morning," said Maia.

"No, it's not. It's ten thirty!" exclaimed Ionie. "Your whole family are asleep. I knocked on the door for ages, and when no one answered I shadow-travelled in."

Maia rubbed her eyes. "We've all got this weird bug."

"You and nearly everyone else in Westcombe," said Ionie. "Honestly, it's like a ghost town today. There's hardly anyone out in the streets. It's like everyone's under a spell—" She broke off. "Oh no!" Her eyes flew to Maia's.

"What?" said Maia, her foggy brain trying to keep up.

"This isn't a bug," breathed Ionie. "It's dark magic!"

Chapter Seven

As Maia stared at Ionie, Sorrel hissed, "*A Shade has been here!*" The fur on her back stood up as she sniffed near the window. "I can smell the stink of one."

Maia's brain felt too tired and foggy to cope. She put her head in her hands and felt Bracken pressing close to her. "Cuddle me, Maia. If you're being affected by dark magic, it will help."

He climbed on to her lap, and she buried her face in his soft fur. After a few minutes, her mind began to clear. "You're right," she said, looking up at Ionie. "This isn't a normal illness."

"Whatever magic it is, it's affecting most of Westcombe." Ionie sat down on the end of the bed, and Sorrel sprang lightly into her lap. "If this is caused by Shades, there must be lots of them, all over the village. We've got to tell Lottie and Sita. Get dressed, leave a note for your parents and I'll shadow-travel us to their houses."

Maia stood up and started to put her clothes on, trying to keep at least one hand on Bracken as much as she could, but it was tricky to do. Every time she stopped touching him, she felt the energy drain from her and her eyes began to close.

"I've got an idea!" Bracken said when she almost fell asleep putting her socks on. "Remember when that perfume was making everyone want to be friends with Maddie? You conjured a magic shield and pulled it over you and the others so that its magic wouldn't affect you. Could you do the same again now and see if it protects you against this magic?"

"That's actually a very good idea, fox," said Sorrel, sounding surprised.

"Try it, Maia!" Bracken urged.

He pressed close to her, and she concentrated on connecting to the magic current and conjuring a shield. She imagined covering herself with it, letting it shrink and fit itself to her body like cling film. "Done," she said.

Bracken moved away from her. "Well?" he said. "Has it worked?"

Maia realized she wasn't sleepy any more and her head felt normal. "It has!"

Bracken jumped round her happily.

"Let's go to Sita's and Lottie's!" said Ionie.

Maia hurried over, took Ionie's hand and stepped into the shadows of the wardrobe. For a moment she had the sensation of the world dropping away under her, moments of weightlessness and then the ground rushing back to meet her, thumping into her feet. There was something hard above their heads. Maia realized they were under Lottie's desk. Lottie was in bed and Juniper was chattering in her ear. Bracken and Sorrel appeared.

Juniper's surprise at seeing them was quickly replaced by worry. "I can't make Lottie stay awake."

"It's because of dark magic," said Ionie.

Sorrel sneezed. "I can smell Shades here, too!"

Maia and Ionie shook Lottie awake.

"What are you doing here?" she said, rubbing her eyes as if she couldn't quite believe what she was seeing. They quickly explained and, once Lottie heard that magic was to blame, she got dressed. With Juniper in her arms, they all shadow-travelled to Sita's bedroom.

Soon all four girls were sitting on Sita's rug, cuddling their animals. Maia had told Sita and Lottie to conjure a shield that would protect them from the dark magic.

"You should try, too, Ionie," said Maia.

"I don't need to — I'm fine," said Ionie.

"I can help you if you can't do it," said Maia.

"I don't need help. I could do it if I wanted to," Ionie said.

"But—"

"I said I'm fine, Maia," Ionie said sharply.

Maia let the subject drop. She really felt it

would be safer for Ionie to have a magic shield around her but right now they didn't have time for an argument.

"I don't understand why the magic isn't affecting you," Lottie said.

"There isn't a Shade in Ionie's house," said Sorrel. "I would have smelled it."

"So that means the Shades must be in something that me, Sita and Lottie have and Ionie doesn't," said Maia.

"We started feeling strange yesterday," said Lottie. "And it was when I woke up then that I had my weird feeling something bad was going to happen."

"I had my first magic dream that night – after the garden walkabout," said Maia.

"The garden walkabout!" said Sita. "Everything started after that. The Shades must be in something we got then."

"What did you all get that I didn't?" said Ionie.

Maia thought back. "We all had garden walkabout passes."

"I threw mine in a recycling bin on the way home," said Lottie. "So it can't be that. The pine-cone animals!" she said suddenly.

"No, it wasn't those," said Sita. "We all bought one."

"But then I lost mine," Ionie reminded her.

They looked at one another.

"Auntie Mabel made them," breathed Maia. "Maybe she's doing bad magic again."

"Where's your animal, Sita?" Willow said quickly.

"On my desk."

Sorrel sprang on to Sita's desk where her pine-cone mouse was. Maia held her breath and felt a wave of disappointment when Sorrel shook her head. "There's no Shade in here."

Willow sniffed it, too. "Sorrel's right."

Ionie looked frustrated. "If it's not the pine-cone animals, what is it then?"

"We didn't buy anything else apart from food and drinks but it can't be those things because they wouldn't have Shades in them," said Sita.

"Who else do we know who hasn't been affected?" said Lottie. "Maybe that will help us figure this out."

"Maddie and her mum are OK," said Maia.

"Miss Amadi was going out for a jog when I was walking to Maia's this morning," said Ionie. "She seemed normal. And I saw Lizzie taking down her Brownie scarecrows."

The Brownies. Maia felt as if she'd just been jabbed by an invisible finger. "What about the plant pots the Brownies were giving out? Loads of people took them home. Could the Shades be in those?"

"We've got one at my house. My mum picked it up," said Lottie.

"My gran had one, and she left it here in our kitchen," said Sita.

"And I haven't got one," said Ionie, her

eyes wide. "I bet the Shades are in those pots!"

"Sita, can you go and get the one your gran left?" Willow said eagerly.

Sita hurried downstairs and came back a few minutes later, carrying a little painted pot. She was holding it at arm's length as if it was an unexploded bomb. She placed it gingerly in the middle of her rug.

Sorrel and Willow approached it. "Be careful," breathed Maia, half wondering if a Shade would burst from it.

Willow and Sorrel sniffed the pot, circled it, sniffed it again and then stepped back, shaking their heads. Maia felt a rush of disappointment.

"There's no Shade," said Willow.

"Not even a whiff of dark magic," agreed Sorrel.

Maia could hardly believe it. She'd been sure their guess was right. "So what are the Shades hidden in then?"

No one had an answer.

"Could you use your magic to find out more, Maia?" Lottie said suddenly.

Maia took out her pocket mirror. "Show me where the Shades are hidden," she said hopefully. The mirror went black. "Whoever's put the Shades in Westcombe is blocking me from seeing with magic," Maia said in frustration. She was about to close the mirror when two pinpricks appeared. They grew larger, turning into burning eyes. Maia hastily snapped the mirror shut. "I just saw those eyes again," she said.

"Like someone's watching *me* with magic."

They swapped uneasy looks.

"You know what? I think we should go round the village," said Ionie, jumping to her feet. "Let's see if we can find any clues as to what's going on."

It seemed as good an idea as any. The girls said goodbye to their animals for the moment and set off.

The village was very quiet. Curtains were still drawn across windows even though it was mid-morning. There were a few people at the bus stop, but there were no children to be seen. A couple of joggers and a dog walker went by but apart from that the village was deserted. As they walked down Clay Street, Maia's scalp prickled. She had the uncomfortable sensation that she was being watched. She looked round but there was no one there.

"Maia," Lottie said, "can you tell us again what you saw in your magic dream?"

"In the first one, there was that person I told you about, walking through the streets at night, stopping at houses," Maia said, "and then I was attacked. Last night I dreamed I was being chased by a load of people, and before that I saw a man leaning into a downstairs window in my house."

"Was it the same person from your first dream?" Lottie said.

Maia compared the two figures in her mind. "No, the first one was quite slim. The man by the window was larger. I don't know who he was but he was wearing wellies and a hat—"

Ionie squeaked and grabbed her arm. "Wellies? And a hat?"

"Yes," said Maia, nodding.

Ionie swung her round. "Like *those* wellies? And *that* hat?"

Maia gazed up the driveway that led to Mr Stanyard's house. In the porch, there was a hat hanging on a hook and underneath it a pair of large green wellies.

Maia's eyes widened. "Yes, just like those!" she breathed.

Chapter Eight

Maia's friends stared at her. "You saw Mr Stanyard in your dream? And he was looking in through one of your windows?" said Sita.

"Leaning right inside," said Maia.

"But why would he do that?" said Lottie.

"He must be the person who conjured the Shades," said Ionie.

"Mr Stanyard?" said Lottie. "Seriously?"

Maia pictured the gruff elderly gardener. It was very hard to imagine him doing dark magic but she knew they'd been fooled by people before. "We didn't think Auntie Mabel would do dark magic," she reminded them.

"And he's not been affected by the magic," Ionie put in. "I saw him in his garden earlier. I bet it is him!"

"But what are the Shades hidden in?" said Lottie.

Maia glanced around and her eyes came to rest on some plant pots piled up outside a garden shed. She squeaked, pointing. "Plant pots! He sold plant pots at the walkabout *and* –" she suddenly realized something else – "in both my dreams, I was attacked with a plant pot!"

They heard a banging on a window. Mr Stanyard had seen them. He opened his window. "What are you kids doing there?" he shouted out. "Don't you be thinking about stealing my plant pots!"

"We wouldn't steal anything!" Sita said, backing away.

"And we definitely don't want your plant pots," said Ionie.

The elderly man's forehead furrowed into a scowl. "Clear off, the lot of you!"

Maia tugged the others' arms. "Let's go!"

They ran away, hearing the window slam behind them. They hurried down Brook Street.

"Let's go to the big weeping willow," said Maia.

The weeping willow tree was the largest tree by the brook. Its branches hung down, the tips of them brushing the grass, creating a den inside them. The girls sat round the base of the tree hidden from view by the yellowy-green leaves and called their animals. A few moments later, Bracken, Juniper, Willow and Sorrel were squeezed in with them. The girls told them about Mr Stanyard and the pots.

"My dad bought a couple from him," said Sita.

"My mum did, too," said Maia, remembering the pots her mum had carried back from the walkabout.

"And mine," said Lottie.

"We haven't got one!" said Ionie triumphantly. "That proves it! Mr Stanyard is the person doing dark magic. He must have put Shades in the pots before he sold them."

"But why?" said Sita, stroking Willow. "Why would he want to send everyone to sleep?"

They all frowned. It did seem a strange thing to do.

"He doesn't like children," Ionie said slowly. "Maybe he was hoping he'd put the children to sleep but the magic backfired and now the adults have fallen asleep, too. It wouldn't be the first time someone's used magic that's got out of control."

"Mmm," said Sita, not looking convinced. "But whoever's doing the magic this time must be quite good at it or they wouldn't have been able to block Maia from seeing them."

"Sita's right," said Willow. "Someone powerful enough to do that wouldn't be likely to lose control."

"Well, maybe he did want to put everyone to sleep," said Ionie. "Maybe that was his plan."

Sita shook her head. "I don't know. Something about Mr Stanyard being to blame doesn't feel quite right to me."

Much as Maia wanted to believe they had solved the mystery and found the person responsible, she agreed with Sita.

"What are we going to do?" said Lottie.

"Let's get all the plant pots and send the Shades back to the shadows," declared Ionie, starting to get up.

"Wait, Ionie! We can't just walk round the village in broad daylight, taking pots out of people's gardens," Sita pointed out.

"And before we deal with the Shades I think we should try and find out why Mr Stanyard is using magic and what kind of magic it is," said Maia. "The Shades aren't hurting people, just sending them to sleep, and, while we know where the Shades are and what the danger is, why don't we try to find out more? It seems like something's going on at night-time."

"It is. The Shades are using their magic then," said Ionie.

"It's not just the Shades though, is it?" Lottie said. "Maia saw Mr Stanyard looking into her house last night." She shivered. "That's creepy."

"She saw it in a dream — it might not actually have happened," said Ionie. "No, I still think we should get rid of the plant pots."

"I think Maia's right and we should find out more first," argued Lottie.

"Why don't we camp in my garden tonight and go out into the village when it's dark to see if anything strange is happening?" Maia suggested.

"Camp out?" said Ionie. She didn't like bugs and definitely wasn't a fan of sleeping outdoors.

"That's a really good idea," said Lottie. "If we see Mr Stanyard, we can follow him and see what else he does. We can also go into people's gardens and get the plant pots. We'll send the Shades back to the shadows and, by the time everyone wakes up in the morning, everything will be back to normal."

"All those in favour of camping out tonight?" said Maia.

She put up her hand as did Lottie and Sita.

"It's decided then," Lottie said.

Ionie's frown deepened.

"You'll need a protective shield, Ionie," said Maia, looking at her. "If you're staying at mine, the Shade might start to affect you."

"No," Ionie said, shaking her head. "I don't want to make one."

"You really should, Ionie," said Sita. "If you can't make one yourself, Maia can help you."

"I keep telling you I don't need help!" Ionie exclaimed. "I can do it perfectly well – I just don't want to, OK?"

"Don't be silly," said Maia in frustration.

"Stop being so stubborn."

"Stubborn!" Ionie exploded. "Silly?"

"Calm down," said Sita, putting her hand on Ionie's arm. "We're just trying to help."

Ionie shook her off. "I'm going. You can all sleep outdoors with your magic shields if you want, but I'm staying home tonight." She threw back the willow branches and stomped off. Sorrel vanished.

"Ionie!" Maia exclaimed, scrambling after her. "Come back!"

But Ionie was hurrying away. Maia saw Maddie, who was helping her mum pot up some plants outside their house, call out to her.

Ionie went over. A concerned look crossed Maddie's face. It looked like she was asking what was wrong.

Ionie gestured furiously behind her at the willow tree where Maia, Sita and Lottie were now standing. Maddie glanced at them, and her worried look deepened. She said something to her mum who nodded, and Maddie took Ionie inside.

"What do we do now?" said Lottie in dismay.

Maia sighed. Ionie didn't often lose her temper but when she did it always took her a while to get over it. "Let's go to mine and sort out the camping," she said. "We'll call her later and persuade her to join us."

"She's really touchy about magic shields, isn't she?" said Lottie.

"I think she just isn't used to not being good at something we can all do," said Maia. "She likes being the best at everything. She'll calm down soon."

I hope, she added to herself.

Chapter Nine

When they got back to Maia's house, they found her dad asleep on the sofa. Maia's mum was sitting next to him with Alfie on her knee. He was sucking his thumb and cuddling his stuffed rabbit.

"Can we camp out in the garden tonight?" Maia asked.

"Sure, sweetie," her mum said, yawning. "But I haven't got the energy to put up a tent or cook food for everyone."

"Don't worry – we can sort out the tent

ourselves and make some sandwiches," said Maia.

She and the others found the tent and blow-up mattresses in the garage. Maia had helped her dad before when they'd been camping, but it was more complicated than she remembered. As they fitted poles into the tent and hammered tent pegs into the lawn, Maia had the strange feeling she was being watched again. She glanced around but there was no one there apart from her, Lottie and Sita.

When the tent was finally up, they collapsed in a patch of shade beside the fence with cream-cheese bagels, cans of lemonade and a family bag of crisps.

"I'm totally puffed!" said Lottie, flopping on to the soft grass.

"Me too," said Sita, leaning back against the fence. "Hey, Maia, your cat burglar looks as if it's escaping!" she said with a grin, pointing at the scarecrow. It had slipped even further down the creeper now.

"I'll have to ask Dad to take it down once we've managed to get rid of the Shades and people are back to normal," said Maia, shuffling up to sit next to Sita.

Looking at the back of her house, a thought plucked at her mind.

In her dream, she'd been in the garden, standing about where she was now, but something was different. What was it?

The fence, she realized. *It was on the other side of me in the dream.*

"Having a camp-out, are we?" A voice interrupted her thoughts. She looked up and saw John peering over the fence.

"Oh, hi," said Maia, getting up. "Yes, we're sleeping out here tonight."

"Lovely weather for it," said John, yawning. "Goodness me, there I go again. I've been yawning constantly the last few days and I keep falling asleep in the deckchair. Barbara too. We didn't even get to that meeting about the houses yesterday. Old age," he said, shaking his head. "It's no fun. Anyway, I hope you girls have a good time tonight."

"Thanks," Maia said. A shiver partly of dread

and partly of excitement ran down her spine at the thought of the night ahead. What was going to happen when darkness fell?

Once the beds were blown up, they tried texting and phoning Ionie, but she didn't reply or pick up. They made a load of sandwiches to keep them going through the night and took them outside along with cans of Coke, apples, crisps and biscuits. Then Maia helped give Alfie his tea and put him to bed, her parents going to sleep themselves straight afterwards. Clio's door was still shut. She hadn't even got up that day, let alone gone into work!

We have to stop the dark magic so life can get back to normal, thought Maia as she went downstairs. She wished they hadn't argued with Ionie. It didn't feel right trying to find out what was going on without her.

Pulling out her phone, she tried ringing Ionie

again but her call went straight to voicemail. She sighed. She didn't like falling out with anyone, particularly one of her best friends. She rang again, this time leaving a message.

"Hey, it's me. I'm really sorry. We didn't mean to upset you. Please will you come and camp with us? It's weird without you and we'll need you if we do find any Shades. You're the only one who can send them back to the shadows. I promise we won't mention magic shields again. I really am sorry."

She ended the call and went outside.

Usually it was great fun when they had a sleepover but without Ionie, and with the thought of a possibly dangerous night ahead, the three girls were very subdued. They ate their sandwiches and then cuddled their animals and chatted quietly as the sun set and the day darkened to dusk. From the entrance of the tent Maia looked at the back of her house again. The thought she'd had earlier niggled at her brain. Why had the garden fence been on her left in her dream? Unless…

She frowned, got to her feet and looked over the fence at Barbara and John's house. It was exactly the same as her house from the back. She saw an open downstairs window and realized her mistake.

"I wasn't in this garden in my dream last night," she said, turning to the others. "I was in Barbara and John's. Mr Stanyard was looking through their window not mine."

"Does it make any difference?" Lottie said.

"I guess not," said Maia slowly but she couldn't help feeling that somehow it did.

She moved along the fence until she was level with the open window of her neighbours' house. She could just see two large footprints in the soil of the flower bed, footprints that looked like they could have been made by two large wellies.

"What are you looking at?" said Sita, joining her with Lottie.

"The footprints in the flower bed," said Maia, pointing. "Do you think Mr Stanyard went to every house or just John and Barbara's? And why? People already had the pots."

"Maybe he was checking up on the Shades," Lottie suggested.

Bracken put his front paws up on the fence. "Willow, why don't you go into next-door's garden and see if you can smell a Shade anywhere?"

Maia glanced at the house. All the lights were off and the upstairs curtains were closed. "It looks safe enough."

Willow vanished, appearing a moment later on the other side of the fence. She walked delicately round the garden, her nose to the ground, and then went up to the flower bed and sniffed the footprints. She recoiled sharply. "There's a strong smell of Shade here!" she called softly.

"But Mr Stanyard made those footprints, and he's not a Shade," said Sita in confusion.

Willow sniffed the ground. "The scent's stronger this way." She started following the scent round the side of the house. The others walked alongside the fence, shadowing her as she went through the brick arch that led to Barbara and John's front garden.

"Wait!" whispered Sita. "Let's check there's no one around to see you."

Willow paused as the girls hurried through Maia's gate into her front garden.

Maia glanced left and right. For a moment she thought she saw someone further down the street in the shadows, but she realized it was just a scarecrow. The street was deserted.

"It's safe," she whispered.

Willow stepped into the front garden, still following the trail. Maia's phone buzzed in her pocket. She pulled it out. There was a message from Ionie.

> I've worked it out! Don't go anywhere without me!!!!

"I've got a message from Ionie," Maia said as Willow sniffed at John and Barbara's scarecrow. Maia took in the hat, the jacket, the wellies and the plastic plant pot under the scarecrow's arm and a horrible suspicion crept into her mind. "Willow, get back!" she gasped.

"Why?" said Willow, looking round in surprise.

"Because—"

The scarecrow's eyes suddenly glowed red and its free hand shot out and caught hold of the back of Willow's neck. She gave a terrified bleat and tried to get away, but the scarecrow hung on.

"Let her go!" Sita shrieked. Leaping over the low wall that separated the two front gardens, she charged at the scarecrow. "I'm coming, Willow! I'm coming!"

"Sita, use your magic to control the Shade!" shouted Maia desperately.

But it was too late. The scarecrow swung the soil-filled flowerpot at Sita. It hit her head and she crumpled to the floor!

Chapter Ten

Maia didn't hesitate. She leaped over the wall and ran furiously at the Shade, head down. She was aware that Lottie, Bracken and Juniper were alongside her. Bracken was snarling, Juniper chattering fiercely and Lottie yelling.

Maia head-butted the Shade in the stomach while Bracken jumped up at it, his mouth closing on the scarecrow's arm.

The scarecrow yelled and let go of Willow. Trying to shake Bracken off, it staggered backwards, tripped over its wellies and fell in a heap. Bracken rolled to the side and jumped up, unhurt.

From the corner of her eye, Maia saw Lottie pulling Sita out of the way but then her attention was caught by the scarecrow reaching for the rake that had been propped up beside it.

"Lottie!" Maia cried. "The rake!"

Using her super-speed, Lottie grabbed the rake and threw it out of the scarecrow's reach just before its hands could close on it. "Oh no, you don't, Mr Straw-for-Brains!"

The scarecrow snarled and looked around for something else to attack them with.

Maia's thoughts whirled. If Sita had been awake, she could have commanded the Shade to freeze, or if Ionie had been here she could have sent it back to the shadows, but neither she nor Lottie had powers like that.

"Lottie, we need to get Ionie!" she cried.

"*You will not get the Spirit Speaker,*" hissed the Shade.

"How do you know she's a Spirit Speaker?" exclaimed Lottie.

The scarecrow's voice was dry and scratchy. "The one who conjured us has been watching you through us, the Sloth Shades."

"Sloth Shades?" echoed Maia.

The scarecrow grinned horribly. "We move at night. We breathe our magic into your houses and overwhelm you with the desire to sleep."

"We?" said Lottie.

There was a rustle of leaves and a faint thud behind them as if something had just jumped down from the house wall. Hairs prickling on the back of her neck, Maia swung round and saw her tiger scarecrow stalking towards them.

"Maia!" quavered Lottie, seeing it, too. "What are we going to do?"

"Go and get Ionie. Use your super-speed and shadow-travel back here with her!" Maia exclaimed. "It's our only hope!"

"But what about you – and the animals?" said Lottie.

"We'll fight the scarecrows off," said Maia grimly. "There's only two of them and four of us."

The gardener scarecrow started to laugh, a mean, hollow sound. "Is that what you think?"

Maia heard the sinister sound of heavy footsteps. Looking down the street, she saw a group of scarecrows lumbering towards them. The cricketer held a foam cricket bat over its head, the road worker brandished its traffic cone and the pop singer its blow-up guitar. Every scarecrow seemed to be holding a weapon. Even the fairy was waving its wand.

"Change of plan!" Maia gasped to Lottie.

"Let's grab Sita and get out of here!"

They raced to Sita and picked her up between them. Hissing, the scarecrows broke into a shambling run.

"There is no escape," crowed the gardener scarecrow. "We know you are Star Friends, and we will stop you!"

As the scarecrows closed in, Maia felt as if her heart was going to burst out of her throat. What were they going to do?

"What's going on here then?" a clear voice said. The Shades paused and looked round. A small scarecrow was hurrying along the street. It was dressed as a scientist in a white coat. Maia couldn't remember seeing it during the walkabout. "Having fun without me?" it said. "That really is the last straw!"

Maia frowned. There was something about this scarecrow. It sounded familiar and it wasn't moving in quite the same clumsy way as the others…

The other scarecrows seemed to realize it, too.

"Imposter!" hissed the doctor scarecrow, waving its stethoscope.

"Who me?" said the scientist.

"Imposter! Imposter!" The scarecrows started advancing on the scientist.

Lottie caught her breath. "Maia, look at the eyes. It's not a scarecrow, it's…"

"Ionie!" Maia exclaimed as Ionie transformed into her usual self. She was wearing her jeans and a hoody and had her bag on her back.

She swung round, "Sloth Shades, I command you to return to the shadows!" she shouted triumphantly as they all stared at her in shock.

The red glow left the scarecrows' eyes as suddenly as if a switch had been turned off. Their arms and heads flopped as they stood there lifelessly.

"I told you not to go anywhere without me," Ionie said to Maia.

For a moment they were too stunned to speak.

Sorrel poked her head round Ionie's legs. "Well, aren't you going to say something? Aren't you going to congratulate Ionie on her intelligence and swift thinking?"

The tension broke. Maia and Lottie raced over and hugged Ionie. "You saved us!"

"Luckily," said Ionie, hugging them back and grinning. "You looked like you were about to be scarecrow stew! Didn't you get my message?"

"Yes, but not until it was too late," said Maia.

"Where's Sita?" said Ionie, looking round.

Maia's elation and relief faded as she

remembered. "She's injured. The Mr Stanyard scarecrow hit her with a plant pot and knocked her out."

The smile died on Ionie's face. "Where is she?"

They led her to where Sita was lying. She was breathing but her eyes were shut and her skin looked paler than usual. Willow nuzzled her anxiously. "Sita, please wake up," she begged.

Ionie sank down beside her. "We have to get help. She needs an ambulance."

"Or magic," said a voice behind them.

They turned and saw Miss Amadi standing there with Fen. "Fen smelled Shades and told me that something magical was going on," she said, hurrying over. "She followed the scent here, and we saw the scarecrows. I want to know everything that's been happening but first let me see if I can help Sita."

She gently touched Sita's forehead. Fen rested

her sleek brown head on Miss Amadi's shoulder and, shutting her eyes, Miss Amadi breathed in and out. After a few moments, she slowly lifted her hand away. To Maia's delight, Sita blinked.

"What ... what happened?" she said, starting to sit up.

"It's all right," Miss Amadi said soothingly, touching her arm. "You were injured but you're better now."

"Miss Amadi healed you!" said Ionie.

"I've been practising every spare moment I've had, doing the things you told me to and trying to have more control over my healing magic," said Miss Amadi.

"I'm just glad I was able to help you when you needed it. So what's been going on?"

"The Shades? Have they gone?" said Sita quickly.

"Yes." Maia realized that along the street, lights were coming on in the houses now the Shades' magic was fading. Her parents and Barbara and John would probably be waking up, too. "We'll tell you all about it but let's get in the tent."

"And start our sleepover!" said Ionie, patting her bag.

"You mean you're going to camp with us?" said Sita hopefully.

"Yep, I've got my sleeping bag, sweets and plenty of bug repellent!" said Ionie with a grin.

Chapter Eleven

The girls gathered blankets and sat outside the tent, sharing the remaining sandwiches and Ionie's sweets. They told Miss Amadi everything that had been going on in the village and filled Sita in on what had happened after she'd been knocked out.

"So who put the Shades in the scarecrows?" Miss Amadi said.

"We don't know," said Maia. "We suspected Mr Stanyard because I thought I saw him looking into my house at night, but it wasn't him.

It was John and Barbara's scarecrow breathing its magic in their house, sending them to sleep."

"Could it be Mr Stanyard though?" said Lottie. "He wasn't affected by the magic."

"Neither was I," Miss Amadi reminded her.

Maia had an idea. Taking out her mirror, she asked it to show her Mr Stanyard. A clear picture of him appeared in the mirror. He was sitting in an armchair, reading a gardening magazine and looking very content. "It's not him," she said. "I know whoever it is has cast a blocking spell to stop me from seeing them, and I can see Mr Stanyard clearly."

"So who is responsible?" asked Miss Amadi.

"We'll have to keep trying to find out," said Lottie.

"And then we'll stop them," said Ionie, her face determined.

"Count me and Fen in," Miss Amadi said, getting to her feet. "We'll help in any way we can. But now we'd better go. Enjoy your sleepover."

The girls crawled into the tent and settled down in their sleeping bags with their animals beside them.

"It was very lucky Miss Amadi came to see what was going on," said Sita.

"And that she'd been practising her magic so she was good enough at it to heal such a bad injury," said Ionie. She gave them a sheepish look. "You lot were right. I should have practised making magic shields rather than pretending I could do them and getting mad at you when you asked me to conjure one. I'm sorry I lost my temper. I…" She hesitated. Sorrel rubbed her head against her in encouragement. "I guess I don't like the feeling that I'm not good at something."

"You're good at so many things, why does it matter if one thing takes you a bit longer to learn?" said Maia.

"We still think you're amazing," said Sita. "I don't know what would have happened if you hadn't come to help us."

Ionie grinned. "My scarecrow glamour was rather awesome even if I say so myself."

"Why did you come to find us?" Maia said.

"And how did you know the Shades were in the scarecrows?" Lottie asked.

"It was because of Maddie," said Ionie.

"Maddie?" said Maia in surprise.

"Yes, when she saw how upset I was, she asked me in. I told her we'd had an argument — I didn't tell her what it was about, of course. I could tell she thought I was silly for arguing with you. She kept going on about what good friends we are, and how she'd love to have a friendship group like ours, and that I should make up with you. It made me realize that it was really stupid of me to stomp off like that."

She grinned. "Though it did take me a few hours to work that out. When I did, I decided to come and find you to say sorry but, as I was walking through the village, something dawned on me. While I was at Maddie's, her mum was putting some plants in pots that she'd bought from Mr Stanyard, but neither she nor Maddie were being affected by the Shades. I started to think about it and, as I was walking past the scarecrows, it hit me. The one thing Maddie and I didn't have was a scarecrow. Miss Amadi and Mr Stanyard didn't have one either. I was sure I was right so I sent you that text and shadow-travelled to your street. When I got there, I saw the scarecrows closing in on you and, well, you know the rest!"

"It was completely brilliant the way you got all the scarecrows to look at you and sent them back to the shadows!" Lottie said.

Ionie grinned. "I liked my scientist scarecrow. I think I might make one next year."

"What I don't understand is why the Shades suddenly started affecting everyone the night of the walkabout," said Sita.

"That dream I had about someone going round Westcombe and stopping at different houses," said Maia. "That was the night of the garden walkabout. Maybe my magic was showing me that someone was putting Shades inside the scarecrows while we slept."

Sita shivered. "It's horrible to think of Shades breathing their magic into our houses each night."

Maia remembered the creeper leaves on her bedroom floor. They must have fallen in when the cat burglar had been peering in through her window and using its dark magic on her. "At least the Shades have gone back to the shadows now." She hugged Bracken. "We won!"

"Now we just need to find out who conjured them – and why," said Ionie.

"We can start on that tomorrow," said Maia. "But I'm ready for bed now. The Shades might have gone but it's been a really busy day."

They nodded and snuggled down in their sleeping bags with their animals beside them, Willow with her legs tucked underneath her, Juniper nestled against Lottie's head, Sorrel curled up in a doughnut shape in the crook of Ionie's legs and Bracken lying on his back beside Maia.

"I'm not sure I'm going to be able to sleep," said Sita.

"I could tell everyone a story," suggested Maia.

"Yes, go on," they all agreed.

Maia grinned to herself. "One night, there were four girls and four animals in a tent," she said in a hushed voice. "But what they didn't know was that outside the tent there was a strange scarecrow creeping closer and closer…"

"Maia! No!" Lottie, Ionie and Sita exclaimed, sitting up in bed and throwing their remaining sweets at her.

Maia giggled and flopped back against her pillow. "OK. OK. I'll tell a different story." They all settled down again. "So," she began, "once there were four girls called Maia, Ionie, Lottie and Sita and they were friends with four amazing Star Animals…"

"Best friends," Bracken put in.

"And the cat was the most amazing," added Sorrel.

"They were *all* amazing," said Maia firmly. "One night, the four animals said to the girls, 'Would you like us to take you on an awesome adventure to the magic land we came from?' The girls said yes…"

"I'm liking this story much better," murmured Sita.

"The animals whisked them away in a cloud of bright twinkling stars," said Maia. She yawned. She was beginning to feel increasingly sleepy, and she could hear Ionie and Lottie already snoring quietly. "The girls found themselves in a wonderful place called the Star World. It was full of light…" She yawned again. "And Star Animals … and lots of … lots of…"

Her voice trailed off as her eyes shut.

"Magic," finished Bracken and, with a happy sigh, he cuddled closer to her and fell asleep.

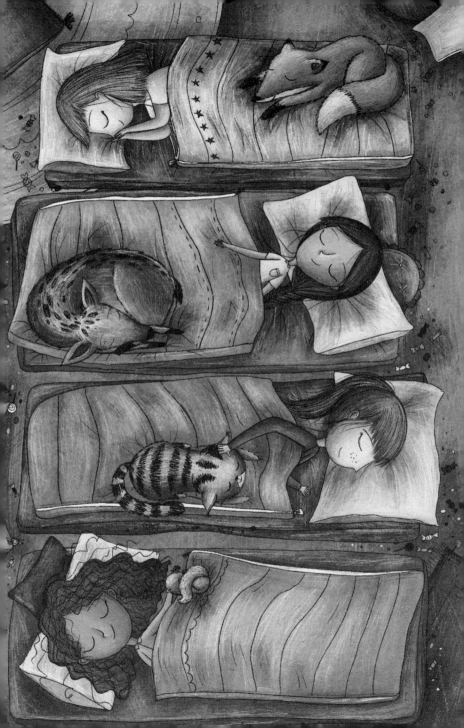

Star Friends
Power Gem

Turn the page for a sneak peek of the Star Friends' next adventure!

Coming soon...

Chapter One

"Can someone pass me a pillow, please?" Maia called.

"I will!" Bracken bounded eagerly over to a pile of them and trotted back with one in his mouth, his bushy tail waving.

Bracken was a Star Fox. Like the other young Star Animals in the room, he had travelled from the Star World to the human world using the current of magic that flowed between the two places. Every so often, Star Animals made the journey to try and find a boy or a girl who believed in magic to be their Star Friend. Once they met the right person, they stayed with them for life, teaching them how to do magic so that they could make the world a better and safer place. Sometimes this meant doing small things like finding something that had been lost, and sometimes it meant stopping people who were using magic dangerously for their own selfish desires. Maia and her friends Sita, Lottie and Ionie thought being a Star Friend was the best thing ever!

While Maia arranged the pillow on her mattress, Sita laid out the duvet, and her Star Animal – a deer called Willow – gently pulled the corners straight with her teeth. Ionie plonked another pillow down on the inflatable bed next to it while Lottie and Juniper – a red squirrel – put a water bottle beside each bed.

"All done," said Maia, looking round Ionie's bedroom with satisfaction. It was a large room but with four inflatable beds on the floor as well as the actual bed there wasn't much space left.

Sorrel, Ionie's tabby wildcat, was curled up on one of the mattresses. She lifted her head. "It looks like we've got everything sorted."

"We?" said Bracken. "What have you done to help, Sorrel?"

Sorrel gave him a superior look. "I have been testing the beds."

"Maybe you should test how bouncy they are!" Bracken's eyes glinted cheekily as he leaped on the mattress, launching Sorrel into the air.

The wildcat landed on the floor with a furious hiss. "Why, you… I'll get you for that!"

"Oh no, you won't!" said Ionie, scooping her up. The two animals were friends but they often fell out, usually because of Bracken's teasing.

"Let me at that rude fox, Ionie!" Sorrel spat, struggling in her arms. "I shall teach him a lesson."

"No!" said Ionie. "We haven't got long before Maddie joins us, and we need to talk about the scarecrows."

"Bracken, that was naughty. Say sorry," said Maia.

"I'm sorry, Sorrel," Bracken said, not sounding like he meant it at all. He jumped into Maia's arms. "But it was fun!" he whispered into her ear.

Looking into his sparkling indigo eyes, Maia couldn't stop the grin that spread across her face. She had been Bracken's Star Friend for almost a whole year now, and she simply couldn't imagine life without him.

Sita took her cardigan off. "When's Maddie getting here?"

"Any minute," said Lottie. "Oooh, I like that," she added, pointing to the delicate henna inking on Sita's arm. "Did you get it done at the wedding?"

Sita nodded. "Yes, and these," she said,

showing them her beautifully painted red nails. She'd spent the last three days at her auntie and uncle's house as the family celebrated the wedding of her cousin, Meera. "The wedding was really fun! All my family were there, there was dancing, a load of different ceremonies and lots of yummy food. You'd have loved it! It's good to be back though. Have you found out any more about the person who put the Shades in the scarecrows?"

"No," said Maia. "We've still got no idea who did it."

A few days ago, there had been a scarecrow competition in their village and someone had used dark magic to conjure Shades and trap them in the scarecrows. Shades were evil spirits from the shadows. There were many different kinds – Fear Shades; Mirror Shades; Wish Shades… The one thing they all had in common was that, when they came into contact with humans, they made horrible things happen or caused people to behave in strange ways. The Shades in the scarecrows had been Sloth Shades that had made everyone very sluggish.

Maia and the others had managed to send the Sloth Shades back to the shadows but they hadn't worked out who had conjured them in the first place — or why.

"Those scarecrows were horrible," said Sita, kneeling on the floor to stroke Willow.

Hearing a crackling, dry laugh, they swung round. A scarecrow dressed as a gardener was standing by the bedroom door.

Sita and Lottie gasped, and for one wild moment Maia felt a stab of pure fear before she realized what was happening. "Ionie!" she exclaimed, throwing her pillow at the scarecrow. "*Don't!*"

The scarecrow creased up laughing. The air around it shimmered, and suddenly Ionie was standing in its place. When she connected to the current of Star Magic that ran between the human world and the Star World, Ionie was able to cast glamours – making herself or objects appear completely different.

"That was brilliant! You all looked like you were about to die of fright!" she giggled.

"Not funny!" said Lottie indignantly.

Ionie grinned. "Oh, but it was. So where were we? We need to work out who conjured the Shades."

"And what kind of magic they're using," said Maia. It was possible to do magic using plants, crystals, potions or spells.

"What I don't get is why anyone would want to send people to sleep," said Lottie.

Maia's phone pinged, and she checked the screen. "Maddie's just got here. Let's talk about this more tomorrow."

The others nodded. Maddie Taylor had moved into Westcombe four months ago

and they really liked her but she wasn't a
Star Friend so they couldn't speak about Star
Magic in front of her. The Star World had
to stay secret. The only other Star Friend in
Westcombe was a young teacher at their old
primary school, Miss Amadi. The girls had
been helping her learn how to use Star Magic
properly but she was away on holiday at the
moment.

"We'd better leave you," said Bracken.

"OK. We'll see you tomorrow in the
clearing," said Maia.

Bracken licked her nose. "Have a fun
sleepover. I'll miss you."

She hugged him. "I'll miss you, too."

The four animals vanished, leaving just
a faint swirl of glittering stars behind them that
faded almost immediately.

Ionie's dad called up the stairs. "Maddie's
here, girls!"

"Coming!" Ionie called back. She looked at

the others. "So tomorrow, after Maddie's gone home, we'll plan how to track down whoever's doing dark magic, OK?"

"OK!" they all declared.

More from Linda:

Mermaids Rock

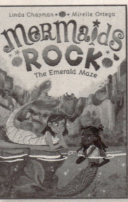

More from Linda:
MAGIC KEEPERS

COMING SOON!

About the Author

Linda Chapman is the best-selling author of over 200 books. The biggest compliment Linda can have is for a child to tell her they became a reader after reading one of her books. Linda lives in a cottage with a tower in Leicestershire with her husband, three children, three dogs and three ponies. When she's not writing, Linda likes to ride, read and visit schools and libraries to talk to people about writing.

www.lindachapmanauthor.co.uk

About the Illustrator

Kim Barnes lives on the Isle of Wight with her partner and two children, Leo and Cameo, who greatly inspire her work. She graduated from Lincoln University, England, and has drawn ever since she was a young child.

www.kimmariaillustration.com